I0158939

THE DELICACY OF THE DIRT

Camille Johnson

To Jeezy and Bubbles.

FOREWORD FROM THE AUTHOR

This collection of poems is a result of a lifetime of writing in journals when no one was looking. Feeling very grateful after getting through a particularly long, rough time, I decided that moving forward, nothing could be as bad as what I'd experienced previously. I decided that everything, the good, the bad, and the mindlessly banal, could be a poem, if I looked hard enough for something to appreciate. I hope to inspire you to look for the poetry in your pile of laundry and to appreciate the delicacy of the dirt.

<u>THE DELICACY OF THE DIRT</u>
What if,
instead of cringing
at the mud
on our feet,
our hands,
our souls,
we marveled
in wonder at
the delicacy of the dirt.

<u>JUMP</u>
Precariously perched.
The edge, a mystery.
Discover it now.

BACKWARDS
Some people want
to go back,
I can't get far enough away
from the past.
There's nothing
I want to see again,
all that darkness
would suck me in,
and I'd never get out.

<u>NIGHTS TO REMEMBER</u>
Hurry!
Gulping down the last
of the red plastic cup's
contents,
as your roommate flies down the stairs
ahead of you.
Perfectly straightened hair,
lined eyes,
and shiny lips,
top off a dress you're not quite sure
is long enough.
Both of you fall into
the backseat of her new guy's car,
giggling, tipsy,
and not exactly sure where you're
going,
other than it's
"downtown somewhere".
Strange guys with stranger pick up
lines,
drinks that are $8 a piece
(and disgusting),
and sticking together,
even in line for the bathroom.

A cab ride home,
(the new guy didn't work out)
hoarse already from screaming
along with the band,
sweaty and missing an earring,
and recounting every crazy thing
that happened.
Falling out of the cab
and up the stairs,
as quietly as possible.
Yanking open the fridge
and grabbing the first
edible thing you see.
Collapsing into an
exhausted, happy heap
on the couch.

<u>THE BRACELET</u>
Criss, cross.
Under, over.
The threads of life
are more than
black and white,
marigold,
grey,
violet,
blood red,
and every color
in between.
A bracelet you wear,
but didn't make,
didn't know how to make,
and don't know when
the threads will break.

THE FIRST TIME

Breathe in, breathe out.
Measured breaths to keep
your heart from pounding
too loudly.
3 drinks-
before,
during,
and after dinner.
Both hyper aware,
of what happens next.
An innocent (?) pressing together
of bodies,
one piece of clothing
taken off at a time.
Make it special.
You'll remember this...
won't you?
Polite, gentle, soft, supple.
Pushing your hair back,
kisses with eyes closed,
feeling his fingertips.
A sharp breath,
awkward shifting,
tender pain,
fitting together.
Sweet, gentle,
And it's over.

<u>IN THE SKY</u>
The changing morning light.
Dark one moment,
light the next.
A human's soul in the sky.

GRACE
Mistakes, unseen-
Do they count?
If you don't know,
do they exist?
Is a confession a guarantee?
And of what?
Fight?
Flight?
Forgiveness.
Omnipresent eyes,
seeing everything,
and still forgiving
everything,
if you ask.
Grace.

THE LAST TIME

Tears stinging your eyelids.
Your throat, hoarse and raw.
Jaded thinking.
Drinks, too many to count,
fill up the new emptiness.
No longer biting your tongue,
there's nothing left to say.
A rough, wiping away of tears
turns into a rough, hard,
pressing together of bodies.
Clothes,
pushed up and over.
Fitting together without a thought.
If it's so easy,
why does it hurt so bad?

THE GAP BETWEEN
A bright, red cardinal
flies by,
on the way to hear another
one's confession,
no doubt.
You catch it
out the corner
of your eye and
smile to yourself
as you watch it bridge
the gap between
up there and down here.

A RANDOM TUESDAY

It was
a random Tuesday night,
a work week
that wouldn't end.
Like every Tuesday,
tacos and margaritas,
except this time,
instead of
"Will you pass me the salsa?",
it was
"Will you marry me?".
Needless to say,
I dropped my chip.

<u>WAIT</u>
Wait for me.
My heart is out of breath.
It can't keep up with
the pounding of you
pulling away.
Ribbons of road between us,
thousands of heavy footsteps,
and the sound of your voice
takes me to you,
in an instant.
The smell of you,
the feel of you,
surrounds me when I feel lonely,
and I live to see you again.

<u>DAD</u>
Strong shoulders
you sat on to see the world.
The same shoulders shrugged
and said "Sure" when I asked
for anything.
Rough, calloused hands
and a smooth, deep baritone.
Whiskey and cigarettes,
lullabies and Goodnight,
Moon.
3/22/12

<u>RUN</u>
Running as fast as you can.
Breathing, panting-
hard and heavy.
Stretch,
reach,
rinse,
repeat.
The finish line,
a mirage,
shimmering,
glistening,
now you see it,
now you don't.

THE LITTLE THINGS

It was a warm breeze on a February
night,
sunset lasting a little longer
than it was supposed to.
It was finding money in a coat
you wore last year,
and fitting into a dress
you'd put into the donate pile.
Running into a long lost friend
in the cereal aisle,
and the hour long conversation
that ensued between grocery carts.
It's finding two lines in a book
that say what your voice
has been struggling to.
It's walking out to your car
right when the parking meter clicks
to 0 minutes.
It's a cheap bottle of wine
with a pretty label.
When a surprise party goes off
without a hitch.
It's your team winning
by one point,
and the whole crowd singing
the fight song, all at once.

When your hair and outfit
look as good in pictures
as they did in the mirror.
It's a jeans and white shirt combo,
and warm potato soup on a cold night.
It's a magazine in the mailbox
and an ice-cold coke in August.

<u>NEED</u>
Air and water.
Food.
Touch.
Touch, most of all.
(Or else one withers away.)
An unwatered garden.

THE BEGINNING

Stolen kisses,
hiding full on make out sessions
in the hallway,
before we told our friends
about "us".
Sitting in your lap while
watching the game at a sports bar,
because where else would I sit?
A love pat on the butt,
every time I walked by.
Fearlessly trying everything
you said you never would,
just to impress him.
Skipping class to lay around
and daydream
about "one day".
Fitting most of our belongings
into a plastic set of drawers.
Deciding whether our extra
$40 a week
would be better spent on groceries,
or memories we'd never forget.
Wearing his hockey jersey to bed,
because I couldn't get enough of him.
Never having enough money
to do anything,

and finding it a fun adventure,
rather than a bad thing.
Holding hands while in line
at McDonalds
(the only place we could afford).
Waiting up to see each other
after work.
Saving him the last bite of food.
Taking 50 thousand pictures together
because you wanted to see what
the magic you felt,
looked like.
Disbelief that your dreams
had come true.

POETRY
Words,
scattered helplessly,
in your mind,
end up
strewn carelessly
across the page.
A verbal nudity.

MRRIAGE B.B. (BEFORE BABY)

The simple band slips
around your bony finger,
nestled up against
it's shiny big brother.
Your body taking up
less room than normal,
it had to be taut and tight
to glide seamlessly
under the layers of smooth,
unforgiving, ivory French silk.
Introducing him as
"my husband"
still makes you giggle
like a fifth grader.
Holding hands
and copping a feel
as you consciously pick out
fresh, leafy produce and
steaming, hot empanadas
at the Farmer's Market
on sunny, Saturday mornings.
Going home a long, lazy day of
cooking, home repair shows,
sex and crisp white wine.
He was yours and you were his
before the vows,
but now it's an official dream,
signed in ink,
instead of written in the sand.

BLANK CANVAS
A fresh start.
Every day,
unblemished,
still perfect.
A blank canvas,
an unopened present.
Early morning,
sunrise salvation.

<u>FAST FORWARD</u>
Fast forward yet slow motion,
a brainless hamster,
running, and running, and running—
to nowhere.
The same action,
over and over again—
insanity?
Or invisible progress?

<u>YOU</u>
Sweat soaked,
muskiness.
The sandpaper scratch
of whiskers.
Curled unnaturally in a space
that fits only me.
Wrapped up in you,
in us.
A knot I never want to untangle.

<u>41 Weeks</u>
A flutter of pain down your spine,
every 8 minutes,
every 5,
every 2.
A rush,
of water,
and a sudden realization
that life as you know it,
is about to change
for good.
In through your nose,
out through your mouth.
Gritted teeth refusing
acknowledge the pain.
Eye contact and a nod
and you know you can do this.
Puuuuush.
And just like that,
heaven is here.

GLITTER
Raindrops on the windshield,
glitter on an evening dress.
A zipper waiting to come down,
a silent decision that makes a sound.

<u>SCARRED</u>
Scarred,
knotted,
twisted knuckles.
Scarred,
knotted,
twisted bodies.
Together —
a fight,
a love story for the ages.

HOME

The salt and sand
stick to your skin,
while the wind whispers
promises into your hair,
"come back for more".
The uneven hem of the tide
creating a crisp,
yet fading, barrier
between you
and what could be.
The worries of tomorrow belong
with the silt,
sand and treasure
on the ocean's floor.

<u>FLY</u>
Once she flew
it was hard
to keep her
on the ground.
A cage on her tongue,
or clipped wings,
didn't matter,
nothing
could keep her down.

MARRIAGE A.B. (After Baby)
Whatcha need from the grocery store?
Are the monitors on?
What'd his teachers say?
How many ounces did he drink?
The dishes are done.
The coffee pot's on.
We're out of dog food.
And formula.
And toilet paper.
Did you check on the baby?
I love you.
I love you, too.

SHOWER
Steam, rises and swirls.
Knees to chest.
The hotter the better.
Water pounding down.
Stay in,
tune the rest out.
When you come up
for air,
you can breathe,
but it means
you HAVE to breathe
it all in.
The good,
the bad,
the ugly.

THE MUSE
Some people
circle the globe,
explore exotic,
dirt-floored souks,
climb treacherous,
snow-capped mountains,
turn over every stone,
to find their elusive muse.
I turn to my right,
while washing dishes
in the sink, and see
one of mine reading
while the other
plays with his Legos.

BLACK THEN WHITE

Black, then white,
then all at once.
Fingers stretching,
a pinky finger barely reaching
the next octave.
Feeling it in
the back of your neck
and that certain chord
making the hair on your arms
stand up.
A, B, C, D, E, F, G.
Sharps, flats, staccatos.
Adagio.
Allegro.
The music saying what you cannot.

<u>LOST ISN'T MISSING</u>
A "missing person's report".
That title is misleading.
Those people are lost,
they are still here,
just not yet found.
Missing means they are missed.
Missing is you wanting to call them
to chat about the latest celebrity
scandal,
or text them
about a sale on shoes,
and not being able to.
Lost is your ten dollar bill
that got put in a different jacket
pocket.
Missing is what happens
when your baby takes his first step,
says his first word,
and she isn't there to see it.
Lost is your favorite pair of glasses,
hiding under the sofa cushions.
Missing is her not being able
to come to your wedding and sit on the
front row,
because her body betrayed her.

<u>DAILY</u>
Wash,
rinse,
repeat.
Dry,
fluff,
fold.
Over and over,
and over,
again.
A messy blessing.

<u>THE MAT</u>
The mat.
A safe place.
Your foam confessional.
Cow.
Cat.
Chataranga.
Downward dog.
Words that transport you
to a different place.
A magic carpet ride.
Dim lights hide
the tension you came to lose.
Incense drifting
into draped windows.
Close your eyes,
open your mind,
your chest,
your heart.
Stretch,
shake,
now hold it,
hold it,
hold it,
release.
Now you're hOMe.

THE PROCESS

The well,
normally overflowing,
with crystal clear,
ice cold, water,
occasionally runs dry.
You dig,
and dig,
and dig,
still deeper,
but continue to thirst,
to death.
With a swollen tongue,
parched lips,
and a dry heart,
you sink into
thirsty despair,
only to find yourself
looking up,
at the rain.

PAPER LOVER
Wandering through the shelves,
15 minutes before close.
The smell of old pages
a perfume that can't be bottled.
Running your fingers mindlessly
over the spines,
waiting until 1 (or 2..or 3)
catches your eye.
Finally choosing a lover
(it doesn't last long enough,
it never does),
wrapping your arms around it,
looking forward to
crawling in bed with it,
and a glass of wine,
the minute you get home.

<u>HE CARED</u>
Whispering,
"But, I love you?",
to his back,
as he sleeps,
on his side,
as far away
from you,
as possible.
Not knowing
he cared,
until he did.

DOWN HERE
It's taking your hat off
during your Daddy's prayer
over lunch,
a blessing your whole family
could say by heart.
A Lenox deviled egg plate
and secret recipe,
passed down between generations
(don't forget the relish).
It's wearing your prettiest
Lilly dress to the Junior League
meeting,
and mascara to the grocery store
in case you see someone you know
(you will), and your
mud-covered boots and ripped blue jeans
to your Grandparents' house
down in the country.
It's playing hide-and-seek
under the Magnolia tree,
outside in December,
the occasional 80 degrees and sunburn
in February,
and knowing how to keep
your makeup from melting
when it's 105 in July.

<u>THE RIVER</u>
Branches dangle,
lazily trailing
leaf-topped fingertips
across a rippled,
glass surface.
It only flows
one way.

SOMEONE ELSE'S PRAYER

The things you
curse over,
lose patience with,
stub your toe on,
and shake your fist at,
are all things
someone else
is praying for.

ALONE
I want to
drive to the beach,
alone,
windows down,
music blaring,
hair flying,
and wind up in a cheap,
oceanfront motel room,
with old salty curtains
and a sandy floor,
drink red wine,
talk to no one,
and write until
the waves stop crashing.

MOTHERHOOD
Your body folded up
like a content cat
in my arms
and your soft cheeks
snuggled between my chin
and my heart,
breathing in that
sweet baby smell.
This is the
unspoken poetry
of motherhood.

TRANSPORTED
A deep
bite
into a
round,
juicy,
ripe pear,
with the
sweet juice
rolling down
your chin,
transports you
someplace else
entirely.

REGRET
A crow,
black as night,
and shiny as
a calm lake's surface,
screams his judgement
from a green, leafy branch,
reminding you
of all the things you wish
you'd never done.

<u>BY HER SIDE</u>
Forever by her side,
a silent confidante,
who won't spill secrets
or cast judgement.
It's leather cover,
scuffed and battered,
holds inside
her innermost secrets.
A portal to her world.

<u>A KITE</u>
Contentment is a kite,
pulling against you,
it's brightly colored tails
elusively waving down at you,
as you hold it
as tightly as you can,
while still admiring
how beautiful
it looks up there.
Don't let it
touch the ground,
don't let go.

www.ingramcontent.com/pod-product-compliance
Lightning Source LLC
Chambersburg PA
CBHW060541030426
42337CB00021B/4376